ISBN 978-0-243-21194-4
PIBN 10548481

This book is a reproduction of an important historical work. Forgotten Books uses
state-of-the-art technology to digitally reconstruct the work, preserving the original format
whilst repairing imperfections present in the aged copy. In rare cases, an imperfection in
the original, such as a blemish or missing page, may be replicated in our edition. We do,
however, repair the vast majority of imperfections successfully; any imperfections that
remain are intentionally left to preserve the state of such historical works.

1 MONTH OF
FREE
READING

at

www.ForgottenBooks.com

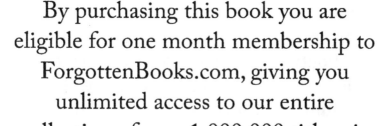

By purchasing this book you are eligible for one month membership to ForgottenBooks.com, giving you unlimited access to our entire collection of over 1,000,000 titles via our web site and mobile apps.

To claim your free month visit:

www.forgottenbooks.com/free548481

English
Français
Deutsche
Italiano
Español
Português

www.forgottenbooks.com

Mythology Photography **Fiction**
Fishing Christianity **Art** Cooking
Essays Buddhism Freemasonry
Medicine **Biology** Music **Ancient**
Egypt Evolution Carpentry Physics
Dance Geology **Mathematics** Fitness
Shakespeare **Folklore** Yoga Marketing
Confidence Immortality Biographies
Poetry **Psychology** Witchcraft
Electronics Chemistry History **Law**
Accounting **Philosophy** Anthropology
Alchemy Drama Quantum Mechanics
Atheism Sexual Health **Ancient History**
Entrepreneurship Languages Sport
Paleontology Needlework Islam
Metaphysics Investment Archaeology
Parenting Statistics Criminology
Motivational

ANNUAL REPORTS

OF THE

Selectmen, Treasurer, Highway Agents, Auditors, Board
of Education, Library Trustees, Trustees of
Town Trust Funds and Town Clerk

OF THE

Town of Newington, N. H.

FOR

THE YEAR ENDING JANUARY 31,

1926

HARRISON O. HOITT, PRINTER

PORTSMOUTH, N. H.

List of Town Officers,

Selectmen, Assessors and Overseers of Poor, Rollin L. Dixon, Albert E. Hodgdon, Alfred T. Pickering.

Treasurer, John J. Greenough.

Town Clerk, Stillman A. Packard, Jr.

Collector of Taxes, Charles W. Coleman.

Highway Agents, Lewis B. Paquin, Walter H. Pickering, Fred H. Winn.

Superintendent of Burying Ground, Jackson M. Hoyt.

Janitor of Town Hall, Luther C. Pickering.

Library Trustee, Edith G. Hoyt.

Auditors, Benjamin S. Hoyt, Lewis C. Beane.

Trustee of Town Trust Funds, William L. Furber.

State of New Hampshire.

{ L. S. }

ROCKINGHAM, SS.

To the Inhabitants of the Town of Newington, qualified to vote in Town affairs:—

You are hereby notified to meet at the Town Hall, in said town, on Tuesday, the Ninth day of March next, at twelve o'clock, noon, to act upon the following subjects:—

1. To choose a Town Clerk, one Selectman for three years, Assessors, Overseers of the Poor, Treasurer, Collector of Taxes, Superintendent of Burying Ground, Janitor of the Town Hall, Auditors, Highway Agents, and a Library Trustee for three years.

2. To choose one Trustee for the Town Trust Fund for three years.

3. To choose Measurers of wood, Surveyors of Lumber, Fence Viewers, Pound Keeper, Fish and Game Wardens, Police Officers and all necessary town officers.

4. To see what sum of money the Town will vote to raise for town expenses.

5. To see what sum of money the Town will vote to raise for the repairs of highways and bridges.

6. To see what sum of money the Town will raise and appropriate for the maintenance of the Public Library.

7. To see what disposition the Town will make of the town land and buildings.

8. To see if the Town will vote to raise the sum of ten dollars to help the G. A. R. decorate the soldiers' and sailors' graves Memorial Day.

9. To see if the Town will vote to designate a day in "Old Home Week" for special recognition and raise necessary sum of money to cover expenditures for such observance.

10. To see if the Town will vote to raise $400.00 for the purpose of control of the White Pine Blister Rust in town.

11. To see if the Town will vote to buy a tractor and a snow plow.

12. To transact any other business that may legally come before the meeting.

Given under our hand and seals this twentieth day of February, 1926.

ALBERT E. HODGDON,
ALFRED T. PICKERING,
Selectmen of Newington.

A true copy of warrant, attest:

ALBERT E. HODGDON,
ALFRED T. PICKERING,
Selectmen of Newington.

Summary of Inventory.

Exclusive of Exemptions.

	NO.	
Land and Buildings		$505,407.00
Horses	78	9,635.00
Ponies	9	325.00
Cows	229	12,555.00
Other Neat Stock	20	700.00
Fowls	1145	1,145.00
Vehicles		825.00
Gasoline Pumps and Tanks	2	200.00
Stock in Trade		50,000.00
Portsmouth Power Co.		9,215.00
Toll Bridges		55,000.00
Total Valuation		$645,007.00

Polls: 188 at $3.00—Total   564.00

Amount of property valuation exempted to
    soldiers   3,510.00

Average rate of taxation for all purposes per
    $100.00 valuation   2.50

Amount of taxes committed to collector,
    (including polls)   16,703.72

ABATEMENTS.

J. Manning Hoyt, over valued	$ 7.50
Frank L. Whidden, over valued	8.75
N. A. Baird, tax paid in Maine	5.00
Rosy Baird, tax paid in Maine	5.00
Discount of 5% on taxes paid on or before October 1st	356.60
	$382.85
Taxes uncollected January 31, 1926	$7,361.21

Number of Poll taxes collected 171.

Financial Report,

Year Ending January 31, 1926.

ASSETS.

Cash in hands of Treasurer	$944.90	
Due from State, Joint Highway accounts, unexpended balances, State Treasurer	156.13	
Taxes not collected, Levy 1926	7,361.21	
Total Assets		$8,462.24
Excess of liabilities over assets		9,701.07
Grand Total		$18,163.31
Surplus January 31, 1925,	$12,628.07	
Surplus January 31, 1926,	9,701.07	
Decrease of Surplus	2,927.00	

LIABILITIES.

Due to School District, dog license	$84.80	
State and Town Joint Highway accounts		
Unexpended balances in State Treasury	156.13	
Unexpended balances in Town Treasury	222.38	
Trust Funds		
Amount of Principal used by Town:		
Langdon Library	1000.00	
Demerritt Fund	200.00	
Bonds outstanding, School Bond	16,500.00	
Total Liabilities		$18,163.31

List of Town Property.

Town Hall,	Land and Buildings	$2,500.00
	Furniture and Equipment	300.00
Library,	Land and Buildings	4,300.00
	Furniture and Equipment	2,500.00
Highway Department Equipment		350.00
Parks		1,500.00
Town Water System		1,500.00
Church		2,500.00
Church Furniture and Equipment		300.00
Wood Lot		8,000.00
Old Parsonage		550.00
New School House		22,500.00
		46,800.00

INSURANCE ON TOWN PROPERTY.

Policy for $2800 on Town Hall, including furniture and fixtures in building, expires January 1, 1929.

Policy for $1000 on Church, including furniture and fixtures, expires January 1, 1929.

Policy for $4500 on Library and contents, expires March 15, 1926.

Policy for $500 on Old Parsonage, Barn and Road Machinery, expires March 15, 1926.

Policy for $15,000 on New School House and contents, expires July 7, 1928.

Town Clerk's Report.

Dog Account.

Number of dogs licensed 61

Seven females at $5.00 each	$ 35.00	
Fifty-four males at $2.00 each	108.00	
		$143.00
Clerk's fees	$12.20	
Killing dog	1.00	
Collecting from delinquents	5.00	
		$ 18.20
Amount of dog money on hand, net balance		$124.80

S. A. PACKARD, JR.

Town Clerk.

Treasurer's Report.

Cash on hand January 31, 1925	$624.46
Railroad Tax	238.95
Savings Bank Tax	428.58
Distribution of Tax on interest and dividends	259.01
Rent of Town Hall	47.05
Rent of Town House	1.00
State Highway Department	487.06
Auto Registration	608.02
Dog Licenses	124.80
State Forestry Department	23.01
Cemetery Lots	51.00
Jackson M. Hoyt, water	23.00
Elizabeth Coleman, water	14.00
A. J. Ramsdell, wood	20.00
N. H. National Bank, (rebate on interest overpaid)	62.50
N. H. National Bank, (loan in anticipation of taxes)	1,000.00
N. H. National Bank, (loan in anticipation of taxes)	3,000.00
Collector of taxes, year 1924	6,987.40
" " " 1924	
10% interest	156.20
.. year 1925	8,959.66
" " 1925	
10% interest	2.04
	$23,117.74

PAYMENTS.

Orders of Selectmen	$22,172.84
Cash on hand January 31, 1926	944.90
	$23,117.74

JOHN J. GREENOUGH, *Treasurer.*

We hereby certify that we have examined the foregoing accounts of the Treasurer and find them correctly cast and properly vouched.

JAMES H. COLEMAN,
LOUIS C. BEANE,

Auditors.

Summary of Receipts.

Cash on hand January 31, 1925	$624.46
Rent of town buildings	48.05
State Treasurer	926.54
Sale of Water	37.00
Auto Registration	608.02
Dog Licenses	124.80
Cemetery Lots	51.00
N. H. National Bank, loan in anticipation of taxes	4,000.00
State Forestry Department	23.01
Wood	20.00
State Highway Department	487.06
Collector of Taxes, year 1924	6,987.40
" " " 1924 10% interest	156.20
" year 1925	8,959.66
" " 1925 10% interest	2.04
N. H. National Bank, rebate on interest overpaid	62.50
	$23,117.74

Summary of all Payments.

GENERAL GOVERNMENT.

Town Officers' salaries	$416.50
Town Officers' expenses	259.73
Election and registration	22.00
Town hall expenses, and church	542.99

PROTECTION OF PERSONS AND PROPERTY.

Insurance on Old Parsonage	9.75
Bond for Trustee of Langdon Fund	24.00
Police Department	33.55
Fire Department	31.65
Damage done by dogs	40.00

HEALTH AND SANITATION.

Health Department	18.00
Vital Statistics	1.35

HIGHWAYS AND BRIDGES.

Trunk Line maintenance	405.20
State aid maintenance	1,790.96
Town maintenance—regular work	874.50
General expenses of Highway Department	74.24
Street lighting	13.80

EDUCATION.

Libraries	90.66

PATRIOTIC PURPOSES.

Aid to G. A. R.	10.00

PUBLIC SERVICE ENTERPRISE.

Water System	315.55

INTEREST.

Interest, Demerritt fund	6.00
N. H. National Bank, notes	119.51

NEW CONSTRUCTION AND IMPROVEMENTS.

State aid construction $1,592.48

INDEBTEDNESS PAYMENTS.

N. H. National Bank   3,500.00

PAYMENTS TO OTHER GOVERNMENTAL DIVISIONS.

To State	1,725.00
To County	1,465.02
To School District	8,590.40

FORESTRY DEPARTMENT.

Blister Rust Work	200.00
Total of all payments	$22,172.84
Cash on hand January 31, 1926	944.90
	$23,117.74

Detailed Statement of all Payments.

GENERAL GOVERNMENT.

TOWN OFFICERS' SALARIES.

John J. Greenough, Town Treasurer	$50.00	
Rollin L. Dixon, Chairman of Selectmen	75.00	
Albert E. Hodgdon, Selectman	50.00	
Alfred T. Pickering, Selectman	50.00	
James H. Coleman, Auditor	3.00	
Louis C. Beane, Auditor	3.00	
Jackson M. Hoyt, Supt. of Burying Ground	10.00	
Stillman A. Packard, Jr., Town Clerk 9 months	37.50	
Stillman A. Packard, Jr., fees issuing auto permits	12.00	
Stillman A. Packard, Town Clerk 3 months	12.50	
Stillman A. Packard, fees issuing auto permits	13.50	
Charles W. Coleman, Coll. of Taxes	100.00	$416.50

TOWN OFFICERS' EXPENSES.

Harrison O. Hoitt, printing town reports	$170.75
Herald Publishing Co., printing notices	1.50
Harrison O. Hoitt, printing names on inventory blanks	1.50
Herald Publishing Co., printing notices reinventories	1.50
Association New Hampshire Assessors	2.00
Harrison O. Hoitt, printing tax bills	6.09
Chauncey B. Hoyt, Tax collector's book, Town record book and Stationery	27.20
Stillman A. Packard, Jr., Automobile manual	7.25
Dog license blanks	2.00
Postage and stationery	3.25
Edson C. Eastman Co., Vouchers	7.18

Chauncey B. Hoyt, Stationery	$ 1.40	
John J. Greenough, Postage	3.94	
Albert E. Hodgdon, time and expenses Assessor's Meeting at Manchester	14.38	
Posting truck driver's notices	2.00	
Telephone, Stationery, Postage	3.39	
Charles W. Coleman, Postage	4.40	$259.73

ELECTION AND REGISTRATION.

Luther C. Pickering, ballot clerk 1924	$4.00	
Strawberry Bank Print Shoppe, printing ballots	3.00	
William L. Furber, Supervisor of Checklist	5.00	
Charles W. Coleman, " "	5.00	
Benjamin S. Hoyt, " "	5.00	$22.00

TOWN HALL EXPENSES AND CHURCH.

Portsmouth Power Company		
Electric light, February	$3.11	
" " March	5.07	
" " April	3.81	
" May	4.65	
" June	4.37	
" July	2.30	
" August	2.41	
" September	3.39	
" October	5.21	
" November	5.21	
" December	5.77	
" " January, 1926	6.19	
Charles W. Coleman, erecting sign	15.00	
Frank N. Hammond, repairs at Town Hall	200.00	
Frank N. Hammond, repairs at Town Hall	100.00	
A. F. Witham, Sawing 19½ cords of wood	19.50	
J. H. Hobbs, Insurance on Town Hall	87.50	
J. H. Hobbs, Insurance on Church	25.00	
New England Tel. & Tel. Co.	1.30	
Jackson M. Hoyt, setting glass and repairing sash and window cords and housing wood	43.20	$542.99

STREET LIGHTING.

Portsmouth Power Co., lamp at fountain,
Feb. 1, 1925 to Jan. 31, 1926 $13.80

PATRIOTIC PURPOSES—AID TO G. A. R.

Storer Post, No. 1, appropriation for
Memorial Day   10.00

HEALTH AND SANITATION.

Health Department

O. J. Allinson, 3 Formaldehyde candles	$3.00	
" " 4 " "	4.50	
" " 1 " candle	.50	
Stillman A. Packard, services as Board of Health	10.00	$18.00

VITAL STATISTICS.

Stillman A. Packard, Jr., recording
births and deaths $1.35

PAYMENTS TO OTHER GOVERNMENTAL DIVISIONS.

State Treasurer, State Tax for 1925   1,725.00
County Treasurer, County Tax for 1925 1,465.02 $3,190.02

INTEREST.

New Hampshire National Bank, note	$19.51	
" " " " "	25.00	
" " " " "	75.00	
S. A. Packard, Trustee, interest on Demerritt Cemetery trust fund	6.00	$125.51

TOWN MAINTENANCE.

Regular Work to Jan. 31, 1926.

Walter H. Pickering, Highway Agent,	
part of appropriation	$168.80
part of appropriation	160.75
Fred H. Winn, Highway Agent,	
part of appropriation	192.55
part of appropriation	43.60
part of appropriation	8.80

Louis B. Paquin, Highway Agent,
  part of appropriation $ 65.00
  part of appropriation   235.00 $874.50

GENERAL EXPENSES OF HIGHWAY DEPARTMENT.

Walter H. Pickering, repairing road
  machine $ 5.50
James H. Coleman, repairing road roller   68.74 $74.24

STATE AID MAINTENANCE.

Standard Oil Co., oil for road	$577.74
Albion S. Garland	110.10
J. J. Greenough	26.60
Willard A. Brown	88.90
George Frost	74.20
H. Frink	11.20
John E. Hodgdon	43.40
Fred H. Winn	247.73
B. and M. R. R., Freight on asphalt	58.37
Stillman A. Packard	19.20
S. A. Schurman & Son, street broom	1.35
Bert Parrott	52.47
William D. Newick	145.90
Walter H. Pickering	14.00
Frederick Pickering	35.20
Darius Frink	51.20
George Garland	70.40
William O. Rawson	25.20
Stover Ridge	11.20
E. J. Rand	6.40
Rollin L. Dixon	1.40
W. Beals	38.40
Joseph W. Stopford	16.80
George Pace	12.80
Charles W. Coleman	12.80
Cyrus Frink	6.40
Roy Winn	2.80
Louis B. Paquin	9.20
Archie deRochemont	8.40
Albert Phillips	2.80

B. Corbett	$4.20	
S. A. Packard, Jr.	1.40	
George Allard	2.80	$1,790.96

STATE AID CONSTRUCTION.

Albion S. Garland	$83.20	
William D. Newick	81.60	
W. M. Beals	80.00	
Darius Frink	75.20	
James H. Knox	75.20	
Ralph Coleman	68.80	
Fred H. Winn	183.50	
Frederick Pickering	75.20	
Archie deRochemont	32.90	
George Garland	44.10	
George H. Allard	38.50	
George Frost	46.90	
Joseph W. Stopford	35.70	
William Rawson	35.70	
Edgar Everett	28.00	
Willard A. Brown	37.10	
Bert Parrott	84.80	
Louis C. Beane	68.80	
Stillman A. Packard	68.80	
George Pace	46.40	
Louis B. Paquin	59.20	
Walter H. Pickering	56.00	
E. J. Rand	49.60	
Charles W. Coleman	43.20	
John E. Hodgdon	21.70	
Stillman A. Packard, Jr.	17.50	
Cyrus Frink	24.00	
Albert Phillips	2.80	
Clark Coleman	16.80	
Harry Wendell, paint and nails	4.53	
Littlefield Lumber Co., Lumber	6.75	$1,592.48

TRUNK LINE MAINTENANCE.

James H. Knox	$ 9.60
Stillman A. Packard	64.00
Walter H. Pickering	16.80

18

Albion S. Garland	$ 57.60	
Frederick Pickering	98.80	
Bert Parrott	92.40	
Fred H. Winn	15.60	
John E. Hodgdon	11.20	
George Frost	11.20	
Verne Rawson	11.20	
Stover Ridge	8.40	
William Rawson	8.40	$405.20

PUBLIC SERVICE ENTERPRISES—WATER SYSTEM.

Portsmouth Power Company

Electric light, February	$11.00	
" " March	7.60	
" April	5.50	
" May	6.90	
" June	10.32	
" July	3.70	
" August	4.70	
" September	4.40	
" October	5.00	
" November	4.60	
" December	2.70	
" " January, 1926	3.60	
Portsmouth Power Co., thawing water pipes	40.04	
Olmsted Flint Co., Dbi. Oilskin	14.84	
Rollin L. Dixon, labor	7.70	
Portsmouth Power Co., 2 H. P. Motor	94.00	
Cottle & McCarthy, labor	27.00	
Brackett & Shaw Co., labor	20.25	
James H. Coleman, labor	5.70	
Earle V. Coleman, labor	28.00	
Ralph Coleman, labor	8.00	$315.55

EDUCATION—LIBRARIES.

Portsmouth Power Company,

Electric light, February	$1.15
" " March	1.15
" " April	1.15
" May	1.26

Electric light	June	$ 1.15	
" "	July	1.15	
" "	August	1.15	
"	September	1.15	
"	October	1.15	
"	November	1.15	
"	December	1.15	
" "	January, 1926	1.15	
Library Trustees, appropriation		75.00	
Jackson M. Hoyt, hauling and housing wood		1.75	$90.66

INDEBTEDNESS PAYMENTS.

Temporary loan in anticipation of taxes		
New Hampshire National Bank, note	$2,500.00	
New Hampshire National Bank, note	1,000.00	$3,500.00

TO SCHOOL DISTRICT.

School Bond and interest	$2,400.00	
part of appropriation	200.00	
part of appropriation	400.00	
part of appropriation	200.00	
part of appropriation	500.00	
part of appropriation	650.00	
part of appropriation	200.00	
part of appropriation	300.00	
part of appropriation	2,425.00	
part of appropriation	500.00	
part of appropriation	500.00	
part of appropriation	200.00	
Net from dog tax, 1924	115.40	$8,590.40

PROTECTION OF PERSONS AND PROPERTY.

| W. L. Conlon & Co., insurance on Old Parsonage | $9.75 | |
| Jos. L. Schurman, for bond for Trustee of Langdon fund | 24.00 | $33.75 |

POLICE DEPARTMENT.

| Harry T. Wendell, police badges | $29.55 | |
| Harry T. Wendell, Fish and Game Warden's badges | 4.00 | $33.55 |

FIRE DEPARTMENT.

Myles S. Watson, fighting forest fire	$6.65	
William F. Woods, contribution to Portsmouth Fire Department	25.00	$31.65

DAMAGE DONE BY DOGS.

S. H. deRochemont, 19 chickens, 1 fowl	$15.00	
Annie E. Pickering, turkeys killed by dogs	25.00	$ 40.00

FORESTRY DEPARTMENT.

Blister Rust work	$200.00

Report of Highway Agents.

WALTER H. PICKERING.

Expenditures.

Darius Frink	$76.80	
Ralph Coleman	38.40	
Frederick Pickering	12.80	
Cyrus Frink	32.00	
Walter H. Pickering	86.40	
Otis Rawson	8.40	
William Rawson	11.20	
Verne Rawson	5.60	
John E. Hodgdon	19.60	
Simes Frink	11.20	
Archie deRochemont	9.10	
Albert Phillips	8.75	
Stillman A. Packard, Jr.	5.60	
James W. Carkin	3.70	$329.55

LOUIS B. PAQUIN.

Expenditures.

James H. Knox	$41.60	
Ralph Coleman	35.20	
Charles W. Coleman	44.20	
Darius Frink	22.40	
Louis B. Paquin	69.40	
Stillman A. Packard	12.80	
George H. Allard	18.20	
L. A. Paquin	30.80	
Otis Rawson	15.40	
Verne Rawson	5.60	
Norman R. Beane	2.80	
Walter H. Pickering	1.60	$300.00

FRED H. WINN.

Expenditures.

Albion S. Garland	$39.80
Fred H. Winn	57.15

Willard A. Brown	$ 8.40	
George Frost	30.80	
George Pace	32.00	
W. Beals	25.60	
William D. Newick	28.80	
John J. Greenough	5.60	
George Garland	1.40	
B. Corbett	1.40	
Willard A. Brown	14.00	$ 244.95

Report of Trustees of Trust Funds, Year 1925.

RECEIVED.

From Selectmen, interest on Demerritt Fund	$6.00
From Portsmouth Savings Bank,	
Interest on Demerritt Fund	3.51
" Caldwell Fund	6.43
" H. P. Newton Fund	4.64
" Mary E. Frink Fund	2.47
From Portsmouth Trust & Guarantee Co.,	
Interest on Charles A. Garland Fund	8.68
" Martin Hoyt Fund	4.56
" Priscilla Lewis Fund	4.28
" Isaac Jenness Fund	2.06
" John A. Hodgdon Fund	2.10
" Ann B. Greenough Fund	4.12
" Albert C. Pickering Fund	4.16
" · William C. Garland Fund	2.02
" Joseph O. Shaw Fund	.17
For interest on Registered Government Bonds	425.00
Total	$480.20

PAID.

Jackson M. Hoyt, for taking care of lots for year 1925	$ 24.50
Library Trustees	425.00
	$449.50

DEMANDS IN FAVOR OF TOWN.

Demerritt Fund in Town Treasury	$200.00
Interest on Demerritt Fund in Savings Bank	106.99
Caldwell Fund with interest in Savings Bank	186.54
Hannah P. Newton Fund " " "	134.47
Mary E. Frink Fund " " "	71.15
Martin Hoyt Fund " " "	114.62
Priscilla Lewis Fund "	108.97
Isaac Jenness Fund "	51.88
Charles A. Garland Fund " "	221.82
Albert C. Pickering Fund " "	105.41

John A. Hodgdon Fund with interest in savings bank $52.74
William C. Garland Fund   "   "   "   50.52
Ann B. Greenough Fund   "   "   "   104.33
Joseph O. Shaw Fund   "   "   "   50.17
Langdon Library Fund in Liberty Bonds   10,000.00

$11,559.61

BENJAMIN S. HOYT,
WILLIAM L. FURBER,
STILLMAN A. PACKARD,
Trustees of Trust Funds.

AUDITOR'S REPORT.

We hereby certify that we have examined the foregoing accounts of the Selectmen and we find them correctly cast and properly vouched.

JAMES H. COLEMAN,
LOUIS C. BEANE,
Auditors.

Langdon Public Library.

To the Citizens of the Town of Newington:

The Library Trustees herewith submit their thirty-fourth annual report for the year ending December 31, 1925.

Financially we have been in a position to add new books and other needed equipment during the year.

In the selection of books especial consideration has been given the children and they have found the library resources a valuable supplement to their school work.

We are pleased to note the increase in circulation especially in the books of non-fiction which have been double that of the year previous.

The library is an asset to our Town and cannot fail to instil a taste for good literature in the mind of the Young. We are pleased to observe the interest shown among our school children who derive much pleasure and profit from it. For good books influence a child's character and life as much as good company.

We cordially invite and urge all to visit more frequently and become better acquainted with the books of our library. The reading table contains many of the best magazines and they are within the reach of all.

On December 1, 1925, Mrs. Greenough was granted a leave of absence from her duties during which time Mrs. Marion W. Prior is acting as substitute Librarian.

In submitting this report it is a pleasure to express our appreciation to Mrs. Greenough for the courteous and efficient manner in which she has carried on the work.

We also appreciate and gratefully acknowledge all gifts.

FINANCIAL STATEMENT.

RECEIPTS.

Balance on hand December 31, 1924	$218.06
Interest on Langdon Legacy	425.00
Interest on Langdon Fund ($1000.00)	60.00

Interest on B. and O. R. R. Bond	45.00
Interest on Portsmouth City Bond	40.00
Required State Tax	15.00
Cash from Reaper's Circle	1.00
	$ 804.06

EXPENDITURES.

Librarian's Salary	$200.00
Books	235.96
Periodicals	53.75
Janitor service and minor repairs	64.41
Librarian's Supplies	10.71
Box rent at First National Bank	1.50
	$ 566.33
Balance on hand December 31, 1925	237.73
	$ 804.06

RESOURCES.

Number of bound volumes at the beginning of the year	6,220
Number of bound volumes added by purchase	129
Number of bound volumes added by gift	9
	6,358
Number of magazines currently received	35

SERVICE.

Number volumes of juvenile non-fiction lent	1,615	
Number volumes of juvenile fiction lent	854	
		2,469
Number volumes of adult non-fiction lent	1,715	
Number volumes of adult fiction lent	1,201	
		2,916
		5,385
Number of unbound magazines lent		1,435
Total circulation for current year		6,820

ROSAMOND M. PACKARD,
EDITH G. HOYT,
Trustees of Langdon Public Library.

LIBRARIAN'S REPORT.

To the Trustees of Langdon Public Library:

· The following gifts of magazines and books have been gratefully received for the year ending December 31, 1925.

Mrs. Edith G. Hoyt, American and
    Good Housekeeping   1 year.
Mrs. F. W. deRochemont, five year's sub-
    scription to pathfinder   5 years.
Rev. Albert Donnell, Outlook   1 year.
Mrs. W. H. Howard, Literary Digest and
    Our Dumb Animals   1 year.
Miss Law, Humane Review and
    Four-footed Friends   1 year.
Miss Ann L. Beane, Magazines
Mrs. J. H. Brazier, Christian Register   1 year.
Lewis Harrison, The National Grange Monthly   1 year.
Mrs. Greenough, Farmer's Wife
Piscataqua Grange, Popular Mechanics   1 year.
Portsmouth First Christian Science Church,
    Sentinel   1 year.
Reaper's Circle, Ladies' Home Journal   1 year.
Dearborn Pub. Co., Dearborn Independent ·   1 year.
Several Reports from State and State treasurer
Mrs. W. H. Howard, One book
Mrs. Edna Garland, One book
Rev. Albert Donnell, Bible Dictionary,
    Four volumes, 3667 pages.

                    Respectfully Submitted,
                        HATTIE M. GREENOUGH
                                Librarian.

Supplement to Catalogue.

1925.

PERIODICALS SUPPLIED TO THE READING TABLE:—
American Magazine, The American Boy, Atlantic, Current History, Dearborn Independent, Delineator, Farmer's Wife, Forecast, Forest and Stream, Four-footed Friends, Garden, Good Housekeeping, Granite Monthly, Harpers' Monthly, Humane Review, Ladies' Home Journal, Literary Digest, Little Folks, Modern Priscilla, National Geographic, Needlecraft, New Near East, Our Dumb Animals, Outlook, Pathfinder, Popular Mechanics, Pictorial Review, School Arts, St. Nicholas, The National Grange Monthly, Travel, World's Work, Youth's Companion.

PHILOSOPHY—100

Forbush, Wm. B.   Be Square   174-F7471b

RELIGION—200

Smith, W. Dr.   Dictionary of the Bible   R 220.3-Sm68 Vol. 1
Smith, W. Dr.   Dictionary of the Bible   R 220.3-Sm68 Vol. 2
Smith, W. Dr.   Dictionary of the Bible   R 220.3-Sm68 Vol. 3
Smith, W. Dr.   Dictionary of the Bible   R 220.3-Sm68 Vol. 4

SOCIOLOGY—300

Mellon, A. W.   Taxation, the peoples' business   336.2-M4891
Brooks, S. S.   Improving schools by standardized tests   370-B790i
Welling, B. J.   Social and industrial studies for the
    elementary grades   R 370-W462s

Pennel and Cusack.   How to teach reading   372.4-P382

PHILOLOGY—400

McFadden, E. B.   McFadden English Series book 2   425-M161

USEFUL ARTS—600

Scholl, B. F. edited by,   Library of Health   R 614-Sc641
Lescarboura, A. C.   Radio for everybody   621.387-L5631
Verrill, A. H.   The home radio (how to make
    and use it)   621.387-V612h
Coburn, F. D.   Swine   636.4-C6391

FINE ARTS—700

Lutz, E. G.   Practical drawing   741-L9781p
Willard, W. F.   A practical course in mechanical drawing 744-W6612

LITERATURE—800

Burroughs, J. Locusts and wild honey	814.41-B945L
Burroughs, J. Signs and seasons	814.41-B945s
Abbott, L. F. edited by, Letters of Archie Butt	816-Ab271

BIOGRAPHY, HISTORY, TRAVEL—900

Bok, E. W. A Man from Maine	B-C941m
Keller, Helen. The story of my life, copy 2	B-K28s
Van Loon, H. The story of mankind	909-V328m
Dix, Dorothy. My trip around the world	910-D6421
Chamberlain, F. The private character of Queen Elizabeth	923.1-T8111
VonEnglen and Urquhart The story key to Geographical names	929.4-V8941s
Wilmot-Buxton, E. M. Jeanne D' Arc	944.026-B9861j
Eastman, C. P. Indian boyhood, copy 2	970.1-Ea78

FICTION

Andrews, M. R. S. His soul goes marching on	An261h
Atherton, G. Black oxen	At44b
Baldwin, F. Magic and Mary Rose	B1932m
Baldwin, F. Those difficult years	B1932t
Balmer, E. That Royle girl	B2151t
Barrington, E. Glorious Apollo	B2771g
Beach, Rex. The goose woman (short stories)	B373g
Beach, Rex. The silver horde	B373s
Birmingham, G. A. Bindon Parva	B5371b
Booth, E. C. The treble clef	B63t
Castelhun, D. The house in the glorious orchard	C2791h
Chamberlain, G. A. The great Van Suttart mystery	C3551g
Coolidge, D. Lorenzo, the magnificent	C777L
Curwood, J. O. The ancient highway	C949an
Evarts, H. G. Spanish acres	Ev19s
Ford, P. L. Janice Meredith, copy 2	F755j
Foote, J. T. A wedding gift	F7391w
Galsworthy, J. Caravan (collection of stories)	G139c
Gibbs, A. H. Soundings	G353s
Gregory, J. The maid of the mountain	G862ma
Hegan, A. C. Mrs. Wiggs of the cabbage patch, copy 2	R36m
Hendryx, J. B. Oak and Iron	H384O
Johnson, M. The slave ship	J625s
Kahler and Herring. MacIvor's folly	K121m
Kipling, R. The day's work	K628d

Locke, W. J. The great Pandolfo	L796g
Lynde, F. Mellowing money	L992m
Lynde, F. The fight on the standing stone	L992f
Major, C. Dorothy Vernon of Haddon Hall	M288d
Marshall, E. The sleeper of the moonlit ranges	M355s
Melville, H. Israel Potter, his fifty years of exile	M4971i
Miller, A. D. The reluctant duchess	M612r
Moffett, C. The Seine mystery	M72
Montgomery, L. M. Emily climbs	M767ec
Mumford, E. W. The wedding song	M9191w
Orczy, Baroness. Pimpernel and Rosemary	Or11pi
Page, T. N. The red riders	P145r
Parrish, A. Perennial Bachelor	P2490p
Pedler, M. Red ashes	P3411r
Pier, A. S. Confident morning	P61c
Poe, E. A. Poe's best tales	P75b
Richmond, G. Red of the redfields	R414rr
Rinehart, M. R. The red lamp	R472r
Roe, V. E. The splendid road	R620s
Sabatini, R. The Carolinian	Sa131c
Sabatini, R. The strolling saint	Sa131st
Sabin, E. L. White Indian	Sa132w
Seawell, E. L. A Virginia Cavalier, copy 2	Se19v
Sedgwick, A. D. Franklin Winslow Kane, copy 2	Se24f
Sedgwick, A. D. The little French girl	Se24L
Sinclair, May. The Rector of Wyck	Si62r
Smith, A. P. Kindred	Sm511k
Stern, G. B. Thunderstorm	St452t
Stowell, W. A. The mystery of the singing walls	St79
Stratton-Porter, G. The keeper of the bees	St82k
Tarkington, B. The gentleman from Indiana	T174ge
Titus, H. Spindrift	T541s
VanDyke, H. Story of the other wise man	V288s
Wells, C. Face cards	W462f
Weston, G. The beauty prize	W5281b
Wright, H. B. A son of his father	W933s

JUVENILE FICTION

Barnum, R. Tinkle, the trick pony	jB2671t
Campbell, H. L. Little Jan, the Dutch boy	jC154L
Davis, R. H. The boy scouts and other stories for boys	jD297b
Dix, B. M. Merrylips	jD64m
Eaton, W. P. Boy scouts at crater lake	jEa811c

Forbes-Lindsay, C. H. Daniel Boone   jF741d
Hunt, C. W. About Harriet   jH911a
Hunt, C. W. Peggy's playhouses   jH911p
Mulock, Miss. The little lame prince   jM9181L
Perkins, L. F. The Colonial Twins   jP419c
Phillips, E. A. Black-eyed Susan   jP5421b
Potter, B. Jemima Puddle-Duck   jP851j
Sampson, E. S. Miss Minerva broadcasts Billy   jSa48br
Smith, L. R. Bunny cotton tail, Jr.   jSm611bj
Smith, L. R. Hawk Eye and Hiawatha   jSm611h
Smith, L. R. Seventeen little bears   jSm611se
Smith, L. R. Circus cotton-tails   jSm611c

SOCIOLOGY—300

Badt, E. L. Every day good manners for boys and girls j395-B144ie
Barrie, J. M. Peter Pan   j398-B376p
Harvey, G. edited by, Robin Hood   j398-H262r
Lanier, S. edited by, The boys' King Arthur   j398-L272b

NATURAL SCIENCE-500

Seton, E. T. Two little savages   j500-Se77t Vol. 3
Seton, E. T. The book of woodcraft   j500-Se77b Vol. 4
Seton, E. T. Woodland tales   j500-Se77wo Vol. 5
Seton, E. T. Wild animals at home   j599-Se77wi Vol. 6
Seton, E. T. Wild animals ways
    Coaly-Bay, the outlaw horse   j590-Se77w Vol. 2
Seton, E. T. The trail of the sandhill stag   j599-Se77t
Hornaday, W. T. Tales from Nature's wonderlands   j596-H7831t
Hawkes, C. Shaggycoat (story of a beaver)   j599.3-H313s

USEFUL ARTS—600

Grenfel, W. T. Yourself and your body   j614-G8654y
Winslow, C. Healthy living, book 1   j614-W7321
Crawshaw, F. D. Problems in wood turning   j674-C8571W
Crawshaw, F. D. Problems in furniture making   j684-C8571f
Solar, F. I. Handcraft projects   j680-So42h
Solar, F. I. Handcraft projects, book 2   j680-So42c
Adams, J. D. Carpentry for beginners   j694-Ad18c
Burton, M. G. Shop problems based on
    community problems   j694-B9551

FINE ARTS—700

Lutz, E. G. Drawing made easy   j741-L9781d
Hogate-Grover. Sunbonnets and overalls (operetta)   j782.2-H6781s

Bancroft, J. H.   Games for playground, home school, etc. j790-B221g
King, M.   Geography games   j790-K585
Goodlander, M. R.   Fairy plays for children   j793-G6191
Seton, E. T.   Rolf in the woods   j797-Se77r Vol. 1

BIOGRAPHY, HISTORY, TRAVEL—900

Dopp, K. E.   The early cave man   j900-D7221e
Dopp, K. E.   The later cave man   j900-D7221L
Dopp, K. E.   The tree-dwellers   j900-D7221t
Dopp, K. E.   The early sea people   j900-D7221s
Foa, Eugenie Madame.   The boy life of Napoleon   jB-B64L
Hagerdorn, Herman.   The boy's life of Theodore Roosevelt jB-R6771

Report of Superintendent of Schools.

To the School Board of Newington:

I herewith submit to you my first annual report as superintendent of the Newington public schools.

The people of Newington have reason to be proud of their school building. Attractive and convenient, with schoolrooms large, airy, well-lighted and comfortable, it will provide when fully equipped a very satisfactory place for the education of the children of the town.

Newington is likewise fortunate in its teachers. Although I have served you only four months I have come to respect highly the ability, the faithfulness and the hearty spirit of co-operation which your teachers have shown in their work.

My work has been to aid the teachers by removing hindrances to their work and by suggesting to them better methods in their work.

I have been issuing from the office weekly bulletins comparing the attendance and punctuality of the pupils of the 32 schools and 7 districts of the Union.

These show that the work of the teachers of Newington was handicapped by the lack of regular and punctual attendance. Many parents have shown commendable faithfulness in the regularity of their children's attendance, but too often some parents have allowed their children to be absent for insufficient reasons. The only sufficient reason in the eyes of the law is personal illness on the part of the child itself. While illness of the mother might in an emergency be deemed an excuse for absence, yet other arrangements must be made promptly so that the child may return to school. The weather, especially during this fall and winter, should not have prevented attendance except for very young or frail children and to them only for a day or two. Certainly work at home and disinclination of the child to attend should not be counted a sufficient reason. Many calls on parents have been made to explain the necessity for regular attendance, and a gradual improvement is noted.

An intelligence examination was given to the pupils of the seventh and eighth grades, that the teacher might know the mental ability of the classes and the pupils, and thus better fit the length and difficulty of the lessons to their capacities. In this test the children of Newington showed rather unusual ability and obtained marks decidedly above the average.

An arithmetic test was given to the 5th, 6th and 7th grades. This test was given in the same day to pupils of the same grades in nearly all the towns of Massachusetts.

The monthly bulletins have been continued. A series of teachers' meetings to discuss school problems and the best methods of instruction has been begun.

Believing that the use of spelling textbooks by the pupils is economical of the time of both teacher and pupils spellers have been provided for the use of all pupils of the grades 3 to 6 inclusive. A new International dictionary has been purchased.

The public library has been very helpful to the schools and we appreciate their co-operation.

Through the willing service of the teachers, hot lunches have been served to the pupils. This we feel contributes materially to the health of our children.

I am confident that the citizens of Newington will be anxious to complete the task begun with the building of the beautiful school house and will contribute the money necessary for the proper grading of the grounds and the setting out and care of the shrubs essential to the bringing out of the natural beauty of the school plant.

In order to make our schools as efficient as the people of Newington desire them to be it is necessary to do more than to provide a suitable house and well-trained teachers. There must also be provided up-to-date equipment and books, children properly nourished and clothed, the right spirit of co-operation on the part of parents, and hearty support of the school officials. To secure all of this is the big job of the superintendent. I solicit the help of all citizens of Newington in the effort to bring about this happy result.

Respectfully submitted,

CHARLES N. PERKINS, *Supt.*

School Statistics, 1924-1925.

ATTENDANCE.

School	Grade	Teachers	Ave. Mem.	No. Tardy	% of Atten.	Atten. R. of H.
Jr. High	7-8	*Elsie J. Pfersick	12.7	74	87.4	1
Int.	4-6	Mrs. Augusta Tobey	21.9	70	90.6	0
Prim.	1-3	Florence Patch	24.0	55	93.7	0
		Total or Average	58.6	99	91.2	1

*Resigned, Mrs. Abbie R. Beane.

PROMOTIONS.

Grade	1	2	3	4	5	6	7	8	Total
Promoted	8	5	8	8	6	6	4	9	54
Not Promoted	1	1	2	2	0	0	0	0	6
Ave. Ages	6-2	7-4	9-3	11-1	10-10	12-1	13-0	13-11	

ENROLLMENT FALL TERM, 1925.

School	Teachers	1	2	3	4	5	6	7	8	Total
Jr. High	Mrs. Abbie R. Beane							6	5	11
Int.	Mrs. Augusta Tobey				10	8	6			24
	Principal									
Prim.	Margaret Pickering	9	8	8						25
	Total									60

ROLL OF HONOR.

Attendance.

Pupils not absent or tardy for the year 1924-1925:

George Newick.   Jessie A. Beane.

JUNIOR HIGH DEPARTMENT.

HONOR ROLL.

Grade VIII.

Katherine I. Estey.   Marian L. Newcomb.
Alexander McKenzie.   Joseph J. Nalevske.
George J. Newick.

Grade VII.

Lena Everett.   Paul J. Beane.
G. Shaw Knox.   Burnham Josselyn.

PERFECT ATTENDANCE.

Paul J. Beane, Intermediate Department.

HONOR ROLL.

Edith Hoyt, VI.

PERFECT ATTENDANCE.

Thomas Norkus, IV.   Dorothy Esty, V.
Harriet Hamilton, V.   Edith Hoyt, VI.

SCHOOL CENSUS SEPTEMBER, 1925.

Whole number children between 5 and 16 years of age 74

Boys	44	
Girls	30	

Whole number children not registered in school
and excused   0

SUMMARY 1924-1925.

Value of site and building	$22,500.00
Value of equipment	1,800.00
Average salary of teachers	916.67
Visits by School Board	47
Visits by Superintendent	63
Visits by citizens	139
Total number days of school	173½

SCHOOL TREASURER'S REPORT.

July 1, 1924 to June 30, 1925.

RECEIPTS.

From Town Treasurer and other sources $8,728.94

PAYMENTS.

Paid on School Board's orders   8,308.29

Cash on hand July 1, 1925   420.65

Respectfully submitted,

HATTIE M. GREENOUGH,

Treasurer.

School Report.

To the Citizens of the Town of Newington:

We herewith submit the Annual report of the New-ington School Board:

Mrs. Tobey consented to act as principle for another year; and we were fortunate in obtaining her and appreci-ate her efforts to keep the standard of our school as high as possible.

Mrs. Beane is also with us again. It is needless to say we are grateful to have her for one as interested and glad to serve would be hard to find. Her supervision over the hot lunches is very satisfactory.

Miss Patch concluded her duties last June and we were exceptionally fortunate in obtaining Miss Margaret Picker-ing to take charge of the primary room. Through her un-tiring efforts we feel sure she is qualified to start the chil-dren in their school work.

Mr. Moore resigned to take up his new duties in Ports-mouth. Mr. Charles N. Perkins succeeds Mr. Moore. He is efficient and very much interested and we think we should all feel fortunate in securing him as a successor.

During January Mrs. Rosamond Packard consented to serve on the school board for the remainder of the year.

The hot lunches have proven very beneficial. And al-though the project has not had the hearty support of the community it is hoped that in the future more will be done toward the good cause.

As ever, we urge the citizens and especially the parents to visit the school, thereby becoming acquainted with every phase of the school work.

Respectfully submitted,

GEORGE A. GARLAND,
MAURICE ROBINSON,
ROSAMOND PACKARD.

Financial Report of School Board,

From July 1, 1924 to July 1, 1925.

From Selectmen,

For support of elementary schools	$5,154.00	
For High School tuition	620.00	
For salaries of district officers	59.00	
For payment of principal of debt	1,500.00	
For payment of interest on debt	975.00	
For payment of per capita tax	192.00	
Total amount raised from taxation		$8,500.00

From other sources than taxation

For dog licenses	$107.80	
Sale of property	2.00	
Other receipts	1.86	
Total amount from sources other than taxation		111.66
Total receipts from all sources		$8,611.66
Cash on hand July 1, 1924		117.28
Grand Total		$8,728.94

PAYMENTS.

Administration,

Salaries of district officers	$ 55.90	
Superintendent's salary	150.56	
Truant officer and census	20.00	
Expenses of administration	48.11	
		$274.57

Instruction,

Teachers' salaries	$2,900.00	
Text-books	113.39	
Scholars' supplies	69.29	
Flags and appurtenances	40.05	
Other expenses of instruction	3.48	
		$3,126.21

Operation and maintenance of school,

Janitor service	$435.00	
Fuel	277.49	
Water, light and janitor's supplies	43.05	
Minor repairs and expenses	34.89	
		$790.43

Auxiliary Agencies and Special Activities,

Medical inspection	$ 10.00	
Transportation of pupils	662.00	
High School tuition	620.00	
		$1,292.00

Outlay for Construction and Equipment,

New equipment	$158.08	$158.08

Debt, Interest and other charges,

Payments of principal of debt	$1,500.00	
Payments of interest of debt	975.00	
State-wide supervision per capita tax	192.00	
		$2,667.00
Total expenditures		$8,308.29
Cash on hand June 30, 1925		420.65
Grand Total		$8,728.94

Respectfully submitted,

S. A. PACKARD, JR.,

Chairman of School Board.

I hereby certify that I have examined the foregoing accounts of the Newington School Board and find them correctly cast and properly vouched.

JAMES H. COLEMAN,

Auditor.

The required annual budget of the School Board stating the amount of money needed for maintenance of the Newington Public School for the fiscal year ending June 30, 1927.

Salaries of district officers	$ 59.00
Superintendent's salary	114.00
Truant officer and School census	20.00
Expense of administration	30.00
Principal and teacher's salaries	3,094.00
Text books	75.00
Scholars' supplies	150.00
Janitor service	400.00
Fuel	275.00
Water, light and janitor's supplies	75.00
Minor repairs and expenses	100.00
Transportation of pupils	270.00
Medical inspection	50.00
High School tuition	
(enter contract with Portsmouth, not estimated)	
Bond	1,500.00
Interest on Bond	825.00
Per capita tax	192.00
	$7,229.00

CPSIA information can be obtained
at www.ICGtesting.com
Printed in the USA
LVHW031638281118
598533LV00023B/1157/P